# WORKBOOK 3

## Space Island

T0350565

Aaron Jolly • Viv Lambert
**Series advisor:** David Nunan

**Pearson Education Limited**
Edinburgh Gate
Harlow
Essex CM20 2JE
England
and Associated Companies throughout the world.

Poptropica English

© Pearson Education Limited 2015

**Based on the work of Viv Lambert**

**The rights of Aaron Jolly and Viv Lambert to be identified as authors of this work have been asserted by them in accordance with the Copyright, Designs and Patents Act 1988.**

**Phonics syllabus and activities by Rachel Wilson**

Editorial and project management by hyphen

First published 2015
Sixteenth impression 2023

ISBN: 978-1-292-11246-6

Set in Fiendstar 15/24pt

Printed in Slovakia by Neografia

**Illustrators:** Anja Boretzki (Good Illustration), Humberto Blanco (Sylvie Poggio Artists Agency), Chiara Buccheri (Lemonade Illustration), Scott Burroughs (Deborah Wolfe Ltd), Chan Cho Fai, Tony Forbes (Sylvie Poggio Artists Agency), Daniel Limon (Beehive Illustration), Mark Ruffle (The Organisation) and Yam Wai Lun

All other images © Pearson Education Limited

Every effort has been made to trace the copyright holders and we apologize in advance for any unintentional omissions. We would be pleased to insert the appropriate acknowledgement in any subsequent edition of this publication.

# Contents

## 1 Match.

1

2

3

4

5

6

**a** My name's Katy.

**b** Hello. I'm Captain Conrad.

**c** I'm PROD 1.

**d** I'm President Pop. Welcome to Space Island.

**e** Hello, I'm PROD 2.

**f** I'm Kim.

## 2 Draw and write about yourself.

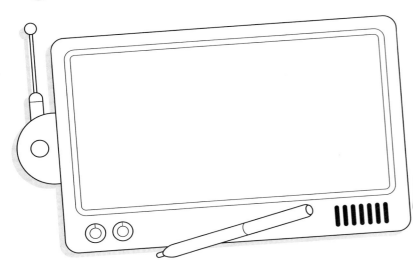

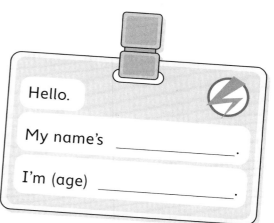

Hello.

My name's _____.

I'm (age) _____.

**3**  **Listen and write.**

①   ② 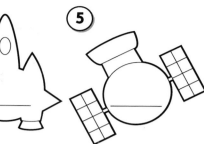  ③  ④  ⑤

⑥  ⑦  ⑧  ⑨  ⑩

**4**  **Listen and write.**

**1** There are _____thirty-three_____ birds in the tree.

**2** There are _____ flowers in the yard.

**3** There are _____ tables in the classroom.

**4** There are _____ teachers in the school.

**5** There are _____ children at the party.

**5** **Write and say.**

| a | 21 | 24 | 27 | 30 | **33** |
|---|----|----|----|----|----|
| b | 33 | 35 | 37 |    | 41 |
| c | 20 |    |    | 35 | 40 |
| d | 10 | 20 | 30 |    |    |
| e |    |    | 39 | 44 | 49 |
| f | 18 | 20 |    |    | 26 |

**6**  **Listen and write. Then match.**

**1**  Boris ____Wednesday____

 **a**

**2**  Billy _____

 **b**

**3**  Marie _____

 **c**

**4**  Andy _____

 **d**

**5**  Judy _____

 **e**

**7** **Write.**

_____
favorite day?

My _____
is _____.

**8** **Unscramble and write the months.**

1. Joe — hcaMr

<u>     March     </u>

2. Jenny — pebmeStre

3. Peter — rNbeomve

4. Ann and Pam — nJue

5. Rover — yaJunar

**9** **Look at Activity 8 and write.**

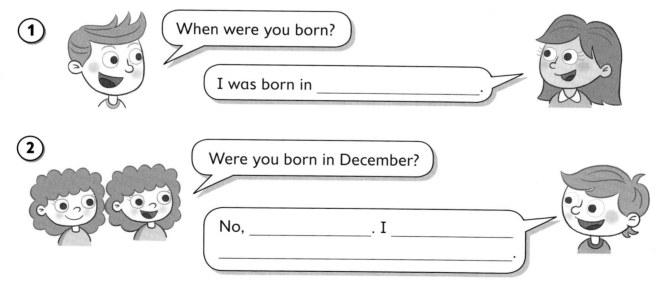

1. When were you born?

   I was born in _____.

2. Were you born in December?

   No, _____. I _____
   _____.

**10** **Write about a friend.**

_____ was born in _____. _____

is _____ years old.

⭐ **Are you ready for Unit 1?**

# 1 Nature

### 1 Color. Then match.

flowers    sun    insects    birds    mushrooms

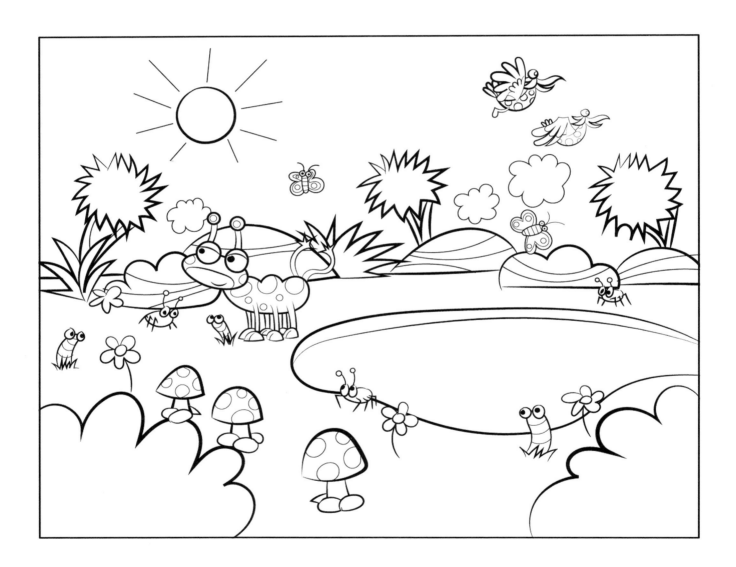

clouds    pond    rock    animal    trees

**2**   **Listen, draw, and color.**

**3** **Look at Activity 2 and write.**

**1** How many ponds are there? There is <u>one blue pond</u>.

**2** How many flowers are there? There are _____.

**3** How many rocks are there? _____ brown _____.

**4** How many birds are there? _____ blue _____.

**5** How many insects are there? _____

**6** How many clouds are there? _____

**7** How many mushrooms are there? _____

**4** **Write.**

ants  butterflies  rainbow  roses  sky  spiders  wind  worms

1 _____

2 _____

3 _____

4 _____

5 _____

6 _____

7 _____

8 _____

**5** **Look at Activity 4 and write.**

1 There __are__ __six__ ants.

2 There _____ _____ rainbow.

3 There _____ _____ worms.

4 There _____ _____ butterflies.

5 How many roses are there? _____

6 How many trees are there? _____

7 How many spiders are there? _____

**6**   **Listen and read. Then draw and color.**

There's a big blue pond. There are three green trees. There are some pink insects. There are six yellow birds. There's a rainbow. There aren't any butterflies. There isn't any wind.

**7**   **Listen and check (✓).**

1

2
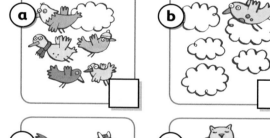

3

4

**8** **Unscramble and write.**

1    many / how / there / are / spiders    <u>How many spiders are there?</u>

2    spiders / seven / are / there    _____.

3    there / ants / are / any    _____?

4    aren't / no / there    _____.

**9** Look at the picture and read. Write *Yes* or *No*.

**1** There's a rainbow. ___No___  **2** There are some ants. _____

**3** There aren't any birds. _____  **4** There are six insects. _____

**5** There isn't a tifftiff plant. _____  **6** There's a pond. _____

**10** Number the pictures in order.

Is this a tifftiff?
**a**

It's small.
**b**

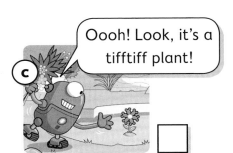
Oooh! Look, it's a tifftiff plant!
**c**

It isn't funny!
**d**

Aargh! It isn't a tifftiff!
**e**

Ha, ha, ha!
**f**

**11**  **Listen and write.**

1 Does she play at the playground? __Yes, she does.__

2 Does she play in the streets? _____

3 Does she play at night? _____

4 Does she play by herself? _____

5 Does she play with friends? _____

6 Does she play in the hot sun? _____

**12** **Write (✓) safe or (✗) not safe.**

 **X**

**13** **Look at Activity 12 and write.**

1 It is _____not safe_____ to play in the _____streets_____ .

2 It is _____ to play with _____ .

3 It is _____ to play in the _____ .

4 It is _____ to play at the _____ .

5 It is _____ to play at _____ .

6 It is _____ to play by _____ .

**14** **Draw and write.**

① 🐜🐜🐜🐜 + 🐜🐜 = 6

② 🍄🍄🍄🍄🍄🍄🍄 − = 4

③ ☁️☁️☁️☁️ + = 7

④ 🌼🌼🌼🌼🌼🌼 − = 2

**1** Four insects plus ___two insects___ equals six.

**2** Seven mushrooms minus _____ equals four.

**3** Four clouds plus _____ equals seven.

**4** Six flowers minus _____ equals two.

**15** **Write.**

**1** I am an insect. I have four wings.
What am I? _____

**2** There are two ants and a spider.
How many legs are there?
_____

**16** **Write.**

**a** 11 + ___ = 13    **b** 20 - ___ = 13

**c** 12 + ___ = 13    **d** 18 - ___ = 13

**17** Read the words. Circle the pictures.

chair   hair   pair   tear

**18** Listen and connect the letters. Then write.

| 1 | t | i | p | s _____ |
| 2 | r | a | t | r _____ |
| 3 | s | e | ll | t _ap_____ |
| 4 | sh | a | ch | sh _____ |

**19** Listen and write the words.

1  _fair_____   2  _____   3  _____   4  _____

**20** Read aloud. Then listen and say.

There is a boy on the bed. His hair is a mess. There is a pair of socks near the chair.

**21** Write.

Crossword: 1 (down) t r e e s

**22** Write.

1 There is a _____.

2 There _____.

3 _____.

4 There are some _____.

5 There _____.

6 _____.

**23** **Imagine your favorite place. Write. Then draw.**

**1**   Is there any wind? _____

**2**   How many trees are there? _____

**3**   Is the sun hot? _____

**4**   Are there any ants? _____

**5**   Is there a rainbow? _____

**6**   Are there any flowers? _____

**7**   Are there any animals? _____

**24** **Write about your favorite place.**

My favorite place is the _____. There's _____ _____.
There are _____. There aren't any _____. There are _____
_____.

⭐ **Are you ready for Unit 2?**

**1** **Listen and color. Then match.**

white mustache

short beard

green eyes

blond hair

( Grandpa )

( Mom )

( Peter )

blue eyes

small glasses

red hair

gray hair

**2** **Look at Activity 1 and write.**

**1** Grandpa has a short _____ and a _____ mustache.

**2** Mom has blond _____.

**3** Peter _____ hair.

**4** Grandpa _____ gray hair and green _____.

**5** Mom and Peter have blue _____.

**3** **Choose, draw, and color. Then write.**

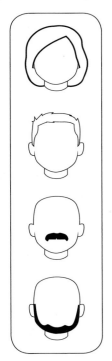  

I have _____ and _____ .

I don't have _____ .

**4** **Write.**

He has    He doesn't have    She has    She doesn't have

 David

 Nina

1 _____ dark eyebrows.

2 _____ long hair.

3 _____ glasses.

4 _____ a beard.

1 _____ blue eyes.

2 _____ long hair.

3 _____ glasses.

4 _____ black hair.

**5**  **Listen and number.**

Tom

Paulo

Arisu

Eva

**6**  **Listen again and circle or write.**

**1** Does ( he / she ) have ( a black beard / a big mouth / a red nose )?

_____

**2** Does ( he / she ) have ( curly hair / long eyelashes / a mustache )?

_____

**3** Does ( he / she ) have ( a beard / pink lips / a red nose )?

_____

**4** Does ( he / she ) have ( a big chin / long eyelashes / short hair )?

_____

**7** **Choose a mask from Activity 5. Draw and write.**

**1** I have _____. _____ don't have

_____.

Do you have a beard? _____

**2** I have _____. _____ I don't _____.

Do you have curly hair? _____

**8**  **Listen and check (✓). Then write.**

He has _____ hair and long _____. He doesn't

have _____.

**9**  **Listen and read. Then write.**

My name is Meesoo. I'm 10 years old. I have long black hair and dark eyebrows. I have brown eyes. I don't have glasses.

**1** Does she have blond hair? _____

**2** Does she have blue eyes? _____

**3** Does she have dark eyebrows? _____

**4** Does she have glasses? _____

**5** Does she have short hair? _____

**10** **Write about a friend.**

Friend's name: _____

**1** Does _____ have glasses? _____

**2** _____? No, _____ doesn't.

**3** _____? Yes, _____ does.

**11** **Read and number.**

**a**  ☐ **b**  ☐ **c**  ☐ **d**  ☐

**1**   He doesn't have a white mustache. He has a hat.

**2**   She has long blond hair and glasses.

**3**   He has short dark hair. He doesn't have glasses.

**4**   She has red hair. She doesn't have spots.

**12** **Number the pictures in order.**

**a** We have Dr. Bones! ☐

**b** Dr. Bones is on the bus. ☐

**c** And she has a white beard. ☐

**d** Everyone on the bus has tickilitis. ☐

**e** And spots?! ☐

**f** She has blond hair. ☐

**13** **Write ✓ or ✗. Then write about Dr. Bones.**

glasses ☐   dark hair ☐   spots ☐   beard ☐   long hair ☐   blond hair ☐

**1**   She has _____.      **2**   She doesn't have _____.

**3**   _____      **4**   _____

**5**   _____      **6**   _____

**14** Write ✓ = good habits or
✗ = bad habits.

👍 Have good habits. Keep clean and healthy.

**1**  ☐

**2**  ☐

**3**  ☐

**4**  ☐

**5**  ☐

**6**  ☐

**15** **Look at Activity 14 and number.**

**a** Cover your mouth when you cough. ☐

**b** Drink quietly. ☐

**c** Brush your teeth every day. ☐

**d** Eat a lot of vegetables. ☐

**e** Take a bath or shower every day. ☐

**f** Wash your hands before and after eating. ☐

**16** 🎧 **Listen and match.**

**1** Amy         **a**

**2** Kim         **b**

**3** Mark         **c**

**17** **Write.**

| big ears | big feet | long body | long eyelashes |
| long neck | long tail | small eyes | small head | wings |

**1**     **2**     **3**

_____     _____     _____

_____     _____     _____

_____     _____     _____

**18** **Invent an animal. Draw and write.**

My animal has _____.

My animal doesn't have _____.

**19** Read the words. Circle the pictures.

dinner   letter   play   say

**20** Listen and connect the letters. Then write.

1   d   i   d       p _____

2   s   a   s       th _____

3   p   a   t       d _____

4   th   i   th      s _____

**21** Listen and write the words.

1 _____   2 _____   3 _____   4 _____

**22** Read aloud. Then listen and say.

Dad has his dinner. Mom has a letter. The girl plays with the dog.

**23** **Find, circle, and write.**

| t | e | e | t | h | p | s | b | e |
|---|---|---|---|---|---|---|---|---|
| u | m | o | u | s | t | a | e | y |
| g | l | a | s | s | e | s | a | e |
| l | n | o | p | e | m | n | r | b |
| o | s | r | a | c | s | o | d | r |
| p | o | t | a | p | i | s | o | o |
| (h | a | i | r) | h | e | e | e | w |
| c | a | r | b | n | e | c | k | s |
| o | m | u | s | t | a | c | h | e |

1  ___hair___

2  _____

3  _____

4  _____

5  _____

6 _____

7 _____

8 _____

**24** **Unscramble and write. Then color.**

1    He has a black (ebrad) _____ and
(stumaceh) _____.

2    _____ brown (lucry) _____ hair and
pink (ilps) _____.

3    _____ a big (nich) _____ and
white (ethet) _____.

4    _____ a red (ones) _____,
green (ahir) _____, and a big
red (homut) _____.

**25** **Look and write.**

Mom

Dad

Tim

Emma

Grandma

Grandpa

**1** Does Mom have curly hair?    Yes, she does.

**2** Does Dad have a long beard?    _____

**3** Does Tim have a mustache?    _____

**4** Does Emma have big ears?    _____

**5** Does Grandma have glasses?    _____

**6** Does Grandpa have a big chin?    _____

**26** **Draw your favorite character or animal from this unit. Then write.**

He/She/It has _____

_____.

 **Are you ready for Unit 3?**

# 3 Pets

**1** Write.

> beak   claws   feathers   fins   fur   paws   tail   wings

1

2

3

4

5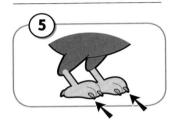

6

7

8

**2** Write.

> dog   parrot   paws   rabbit   skin   snake   whiskers   wing

 We have a  and a . Our [1] _____ has long  [2] _____. Our [3] _____ has green and brown [4] _____.

We have a  and a . Our [5] _____ has brown  [6] _____. Our [7] _____ has one  [8] _____. It can't fly, but it can talk.

**3** Write.

| It has   It doesn't have   They have   They don't have |

**1** What does it look like?

_____ two eyes. _____ legs.

**2** What does it look like?

_____ a tail. _____ arms.

**3** What do they look like?

_____ claws. _____ fur.

**4** Write.

**1**   The rabbit has a _____ and _____ .

**2**   The parrot has two _____ and a _____ .

**3**   The cat doesn't have _____ .

**4**   The dog has _____ .

**5**   The snake doesn't have _____ .

**6**   The frog has green _____ . It doesn't have _____ .

**7**   The fish has _____ .

**5**  **Listen and draw. Then write.**

**1**

The turtle has a _____.

**2**

The cat has _____.

**3**

The bird has _____.

**4**

The dog has _____.

**6** **Match.**

1

2

3

4

**a**   cute

**b**   fast

**c**   slow

**d**   scary

**7**  **Listen and circle. Then write.**

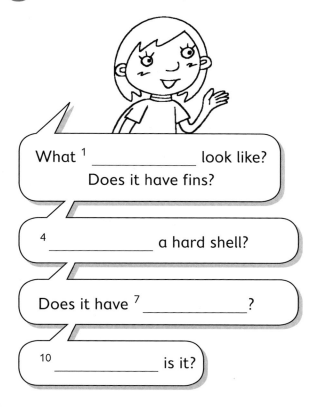

**Animal:** ( cat / rabbit )

**Name:** ( Luke / Lily )

**Age:** ( three years old / eight years old )

**Color:** ( white / brown )

**Legs:** ( no legs / four legs )

**Food:** ( eggs / fruit )

I have a pet. It's a [1] _____. Its name's [2] _____.

It's [3] _____ years old. It's white, and it has soft fur. It has [4] _____ legs, but you can't see them. There's a lot of fur! It likes [5] _____.

**8** **Look at Activity 7 and write.**

What [1] _____ look like? Does it have fins?

[4] _____ a hard shell?

Does it have [7] _____ ?

[10] _____ is it?

[2] _____ , it [3] _____.

[5] _____ , it [6] _____.

[8] _____ , it [9] _____. It's soft and white.

It's a [11] _____.

## 9 Look and write *Yes* or *No*.

Does it have spots? _____

Does it have a short tail? _____

Does it have sharp teeth? _____

Is it the wabberjock? _____

Is it very big? _____

Does it have long legs? _____

Does it have spots? _____

Is it the wabberjock? _____

Is it small? _____

Does it have spots? _____

Does it have a long tail? _____

Is it the wabberjock? _____

## 10 Write about the animals in Activity 9.

1  This animal has blue _____ and spots. It has a long _____ and sharp _____ . It _____ the wabberjock.

2  This animal is very _____ . It has orange fur and _____ . It _____ the wabberjock.

3  This animal has pink _____ and spots. It has a _____ tail. _____ the wabberjock!

**11** Write.

VALUES

Take care of your pet.

| clean | exercise | feed | turtle | vet | water |

My name is Marcus. I have birds, fish, a dog, a cat, and a ¹ _____ . I ² _____ my pets and give them fresh ³ _____ every day. I keep my pets ⁴ _____ . I go to the park and give my pets a lot of ⁵ _____ , too. I take them to the ⁶ _____ when they're sick.

**12** Do you know how to take care of pets? Write the letter.

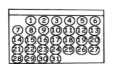

D = every day

W = every week

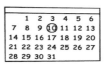

S = sometimes

1

2

3

4

5

6

**13** **Number the pictures in order. Then write.**

**Life cycle of a butterfly**

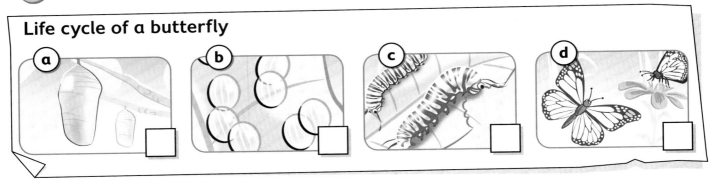

a □  b □  c □  d □

| butterflies   caterpillars   cocoons   eggs |

First, there are small [1] _____. Next, there [2] _____.

Then [3] _____. Finally, [4] _____.

**14** **Write.**

| big tadpoles   eggs   frogs   small tadpoles |

**Life cycle of a frog**

① _____  ② _____  ③ _____  ④ _____

**15** **Write.**

**1** Do butterflies have wings? _____

**2** Do frogs have big mouths? _____

**3** Do small tadpoles have legs? _____

**4** Do caterpillars have legs? _____

**16** Read the words. Circle the pictures.

coin   eat   leaf   tea

**PHONICS** **3**

ea   oi

**17**  Listen and connect the letters. Then write.

| 1 | c | i | k | r _____ |
|---|---|---|---|---|
| 2 | d | a | ng | c _____ |
| 3 | r | n | p | d _____ |
| 4 | i | i | g | i _____ |

**18**  Listen and write the words.

1 _____    2 _____    3 _____    4 _____

**19** Read aloud. Then listen and say.

Join me for tea. We can have leaf tea in a cup. We can eat, too.

**20** Unscramble and write.

skewhirs  ginsw  ruf  tila  wacsl  kins  sifn  aftershe  swap  beka

1 _____  2 _____

3 _____  4 _____

5 _____  6 _____

7 _____  8 _____

9 _____  10 _____

**21** Check (✓).

| | fast | slow | green skin | soft fur | hard shell |
|---|---|---|---|---|---|
| **1** hamster | | | | | |
| **2** turtle | | | | | |
| **3** frog | | | | | |

**22** Look at Activity 21 and write.

**1** The hamster is _____fast_____. It has _____.

**2** The turtle is _____. _____

**3** The frog _____. _____

**23** **Draw and label two animals.**

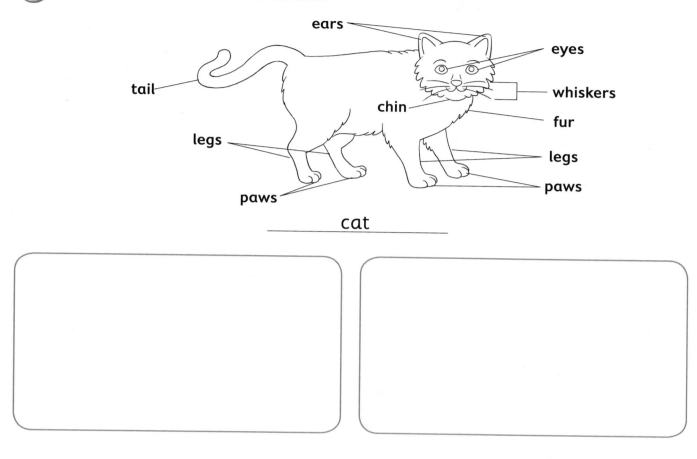

ears

eyes

tail

whiskers

chin

fur

legs

legs

paws

paws

cat

_____          _____

**24** **Choose one animal in Activity 23 and write.**

The _____ has _____ and _____ .

It doesn't have _____ . It can _____ .

It is very _____ .

**25** **Write about your favorite pet.**

My favorite pet is a _____ . It is _____ .

It has _____ . It doesn't have _____ .

 **Are you ready for Unit 4?**

# 4 Home

**1** Match.

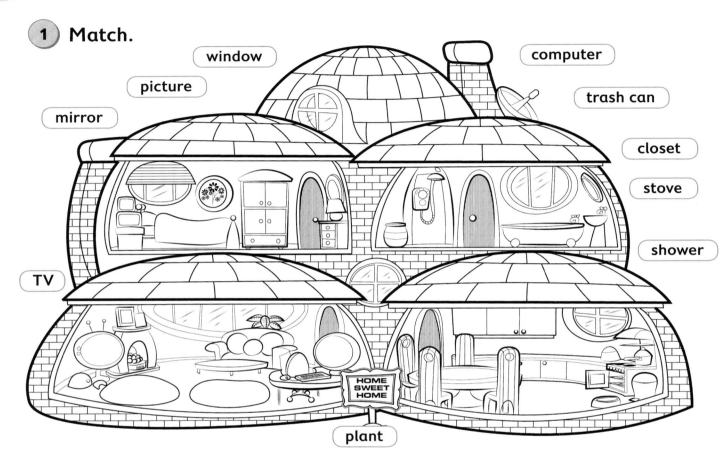

window
picture
mirror
computer
trash can
closet
stove
shower
TV
plant

**2** Look at Activity 1 and write.

above   behind   below   in front of   next to

**1**   The sofa is _____ the plant.

**2**   The window is _____ the sofa.

**3**   The table is _____ the sofa.

**4**   The mirror is _____ the sink.

**5**   The closet is _____ the bed.

## 3 Write *Yes* or *No*.

1   There are pictures in the bedroom. They're above the bed.                              _____

2   There's a plant in the living room. It's behind the sofa.                                    _____

3   There's a trash can in the kitchen. It's in front of the refrigerator.                _____

4   There's a stove in the kitchen. It's next to the sink.                                        _____

5   There's a mirror in the bathroom. It's below the sink.                                     _____

6   There's a lamp in the bedroom. It's next to the bed.                                        _____

7   There's a frog in the bathroom. It's in the shower.                                          _____

## 4 Read. Draw the items in the picture in Activity 3.

1   There's a big picture in the bathroom. It's next to the mirror.

2   There's a closet in the bedroom. It's next to the bed.

3   There's a lamp in the living room. It's behind the sofa.

**5** Write.

blankets   stove   computer   pans   ~~pot~~   table

**1**   Is the _____pot_____ on the sofa?        No, it isn't. It's on the stove.

**2**   Are the _____ on the stove?        Yes, they are.

**3**   Are the plates in the _____?        No, they aren't.

**4**   Is the _____ in front of the sofa?   Yes, it is.

**5**   Are the _____ behind the sofa?      No, they aren't. They're on the sofa.

**6**   Is the _____ on the table?          Yes, it is.

**6**  Listen and write.

**1**   __Yes__, it __is__.     **2**   _____, they _____.     **3**   _____, it _____.

**4**   _____, it _____.     **5**   _____, it _____.     **6**   _____, it _____.

## 7 Write.

bed   chair   in front of   next to   plant   sofa   under

1   Is the hamster in the shower? _____

2   Is the hamster on the bed? _____

3   Is the hamster on the sofa? _____

4   _____ behind the _____? Yes, it is.

5   _____ in front of the _____? No, it isn't.
It's above the chair.

6   Is the hamster under the computer? _____

_____

## 8  Look at Activity 7. Listen and write the number.

a    b    c    d    e    f

**9** **Write. Then number the pictures in order.**

It isn't your plant. It's our plant!

Oh, no! My kitchen!

Do you have a tifftiff plant?

Oh, no! The trickster has the tifftiff plant!

> **has    have    kitchen    plant**

**a**    It isn't your plant. It's our _____!

**b**    Oh, no! My _____!

**c**    Do you _____ a tifftiff plant?

**d**    Oh, no! The trickster _____ the tifftiff plant!

**10** **Where's the tifftiff plant? Write.**

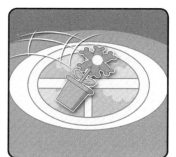
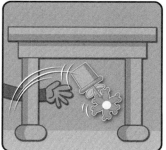

**1**    It's _____ the table.

**2**    It's _____ the stove.

**3**    It's _____ the window.

**4**    It's _____ the table.

**11** **Do you help at home? Write the letter.**

Help at home.

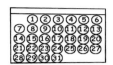

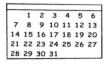

**D = every day**   **W = every week**   **S = sometimes**   **N = never**

**12** **Write *I like* or *I don't like*.**

1 _____ taking out the trash.

2 _____ dusting the shelves.

3 _____ hanging up my clothes.

4 _____ putting away my toys.

5 _____ drying the dishes.

6 _____ sweeping the floor.

**13** Find and color the frog.

**14** Write. Then draw a mosaic animal.

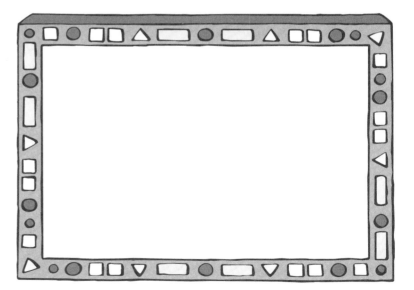

**15** Write three things that can be used to make mosaics.

1 _____     2 _____     3 _____

**16** Read the words. Circle the pictures.

a_e   i_e   o_e

bone   cake   home   time

**17** 🎧 Listen and connect the letters. Then write.

1  ( k )——( i )  ( t )   t _____

2  ( t )  ( ee )  ( l )   k _____

3  ( k )  ( ai )  ( ck )   f _____

4  ( f )  ( i )  ( d )   k _____

**18** 🎧 Listen and write the words.

1 _____   2 _____   3 _____   4 _____

5 _____

**19** 🎧 Read aloud. Then listen and say.

The boy eats his cake, and the dog has a bone. The park's fun, but it's time to go home.

**20** **Unscramble and write.**

1   empcourt   _____

2   oclest   _____

3   dowinw   _____

4   slefh   _____

5   bocm   _____

6   urbshototh   _____

7   epalts   _____

8   ewolts   _____

9   kenbalts   _____

10   sapn   _____

**21**   **Listen and draw. Then write.**

1   There are _____ in the bathroom. They're _____ the sink.

2   There's a bed below the _____.

3   Is there a lamp behind the sofa? _____

4   Is there a closet in the bedroom? _____

5   There are _____ in the living room. They're _____ the sofa.

6   Is there a mirror above the sink? _____

**22** **What's in your dream bedroom? Check.**

**23** **Write about your dream bedroom.**

> My dream bedroom's great! There's a big bed. There's a sofa next to the bed. There's a big TV. The computer's on a desk behind the sofa. There are a lot of clothes in the closet. There are a lot of toys. I like my dream bedroom.

My dream _____ 's _____ . There's _____ .
There are _____ . The _____ 's _____
the _____ . I _____ my dream bedroom.

**24** **Write questions to ask a friend about their dream bedroom.**

**1** Is there a _____ ?

**2** Where is the _____ ?

**3** What's in the _____ ?

**4** Are there any _____ ?

**5** How many _____ are there?

⭐ **Are you ready for Unit 5?**

# 5 Clothes

## 1 Match.

1
2
3
4
5
6
7

- a) a sweatsuit
- b) a uniform
- c) belt
- d) a sweatshirt
- e) a baseball cap
- f) sandals
- g) flip-flops
- h) a polo shirt
- i) a jacket
- j) a shirt
- k) shorts
- l) sneakers
- m) jeans

8
9
10
11
12
13

## 2 Write.

1

I'm wearing a shirt, pants, _____,
a _____, and a hat.

2

I'm wearing a _____, jeans,
sneakers, and a _____.

**3**   **Listen and draw. Then color.**

What's he wearing?

He's wearing...

**4** **Look at Activity 3 and write.**

**1** What's he wearing? He's wearing a _____, a _____, _____, and _____.

**2** Is he wearing a belt? _____, he _____.

**3** Is he wearing a baseball cap? _____, he _____.

**5**  **Write. Then listen and color.**

beanie    hiking boots    scarf    shoes    ski jacket    tights    wool sweater

1 _____

2 _____

3 _____

4 _____

5 _____

6 _____

7 _____

**6** **Look at Activity 5 and write.**

colorful    fancy    plain

1    Is _____ wearing a _____ wool sweater? Yes, _____.

2    _____'s wearing a _____ ski jacket.

3    _____'s wearing a _____ green beanie.

**7**  **Check (✓). Then listen, read, and circle.**

| | | | |
|---|---|---|---|
| sandals | ☐ | baseball cap | ☐ |
| sneakers | ☐ | belt | ☐ |
| shirt | ☐ | skirt | ☐ |
| sweatshirt | ☐ | jeans | ☐ |
| glasses | ☐ | shorts | ☐ |

**1**  Is she wearing a belt? ( Yes, she is. / No, she isn't. )

**2**  Is she wearing a plain baseball cap? ( Yes, she is. / No, she isn't. )

**3**  Is she wearing fancy glasses? ( Yes, she is. / No, she isn't. )

**4**  Is she wearing plain sneakers? ( Yes, she is. / No, she isn't. )

**8** **Write.**

| love | my favorite | These are | This is |
|---|---|---|---|

I ¹ _____ my tights and my shoes! This is ² _____ scarf.

³ _____ my favorite hiking boots. ⁴ _____ my favorite sweater.

**9** **Check (✓) your favorite clothes.**

| | | | | | | | |
|---|---|---|---|---|---|---|---|
| a baseball cap | ☐ | a beanie | ☐ | a belt | ☐ | sandals | ☐ |
| a jacket | ☐ | a dress | ☐ | a uniform | ☐ | flip flops | ☐ |
| a sweatshirt | ☐ | jeans | ☐ | a polo shirt | ☐ | shorts | ☐ |

**10** **Unscramble and write.**

has He tifftiff plant. the
_____

**1**

shirt! at Look red the
_____

**2**

jeans! the Behind There!
_____

**3**

a dress. is PROD 2 wearing
_____

**4**

**11** **Write.**

**1**   Is Kim wearing a sweatshirt?          No, he isn't.

**2**   Is PROD 2 wearing a dress?          _____

**3**   Is Katy wearing a belt?          _____

**4**   Is the trickster wearing a baseball cap?          _____

Be polite.

**12** Write.

> Excuse me   Have a nice day!   I'm sorry
> Please   Thank you.   You're welcome.

1. _____, Marie. Can you give me those buns, please?

   These buns?

2. Yes. _____ put them in the cart.

   OK.

3. _____

   _____

4. Oh, _____, Mom.

   That's OK.

5. Let's go to the checkout.

   Sure, Mom.

6. I love this store. It's big.

   Great! _____

**13** **Match and write.**

| | | | | |
|---|---|---|---|---|
| **1** | set | **a** | the dishes | _____ |
| **2** | wash | **b** | my bedroom | _____ |
| **3** | make | **c** | the car | _____ |
| **4** | wash | **d** | the table | _____ |
| **5** | clean | **e** | the bed | _____ |

**14** **Read the chores in Activity 13 and number.**

**15** **Read the words. Circle the pictures.**

scarf   skate   spoon   star

**PHONICS**

| sc | sk | sm | sn |
| sp | squ | st | sw |

**16** **Listen and connect the letters. Then write.**

1   h   u   t      c _____

2   c   igh   t    c _____

3   l   oa   t     h _____

4   c   a   p      l _____

**17** **Listen and write the words.**

1 _____   2 _____   3 _____   4 _____

**18** **Read aloud. Then listen and say.**

The cats skate on the lake. One wears a hat, and one wears a scarf. The moon is high, and we can see a big star.

**19** **Find and circle the words.**

| d | a | d | s | m | b | e | a | n | i | e | j | s | s |
|---|---|---|---|---|---|---|---|---|---|---|---|---|---|
| b | e | l | m | o | a | s | u | b | j | s | o | k | a |
| s | w | e | a | t | s | h | i | r | t | h | c | i | n |
| u | b | h | j | z | e | o | n | o | e | o | n | j | d |
| n | l | a | a | b | b | r | i | o | a | r | p | a | a |
| i | s | s | w | e | a | t | s | u | i | t | o | c | l |
| f | w | c | c | s | l | s | f | t | n | b | l | k | s |
| o | e | a | k | a | l | q | o | s | t | l | o | e | y |
| r | a | r | e | s | c | a | r | f | i | o | s | t | m |
| m | b | e | l | t | a | u | m | s | g | p | h | w | c |
| s | b | l | t | o | p | u | s | e | h | s | i | x | i |
| c | w | o | o | l | s | w | e | a | t | e | r | t | b |
| f | l | i | p | f | l | o | p | s | s | c | t | b | o |

**20** **Write the questions or answers.**

**1** Is he wearing sneakers?

_____ .

**2** _____ ?

Yes, he is. It's his favorite T-shirt.

**3** Is he wearing pants?

_____ .

**4** _____ ?

Yes, he is. He loves his baseball cap.

**21**  **Draw and color your favorite clothes.**

**22** **Write about your favorite clothes.**

**1** These are my favorite sneakers. They're _____.

**2** This is my favorite baseball cap. It's _____.

**3** I love my _____. _____ fancy.

**4** _____ _____ colorful.

**5** _____ _____ plain.

**23** **Pretend you're wearing your favorite clothes. Write.**

Today I'm wearing _____

_____

_____.

 **Are you ready for Unit 6?**

# 6 Sports

## 1 Number.

1 play baseball     2 play soccer     3 play basketball

4 ride a bike     5 do taekwondo     6 play tennis

7 run     8 catch a ball

**a**     **b**     **c**     **d**

**e**     **f**     **g**     **h**

## 2 Circle.

1 I ( can / can't ) jump.     2 I ( can / can't ) climb a tree.

3 I ( can / can't ) play baseball.     4 I ( can / can't ) play soccer.

5 I ( can / can't ) play basketball.     6 I ( can / can't ) ride a bike.

7 I ( can / can't ) do taekwondo.     8 I ( can / can't ) play tennis.

9 I ( can / can't ) run.     10 I ( can / can't ) catch a ball.

**3**  **Listen and ✓ = can or ✗ = can't.**

| | |  | | | | | |
|---|---|---|---|---|---|---|---|
| Jake | | | | | | ✗ | ✓ |
| Paul | | | | | | | |
| Beth | | | | | | | |
| Gina | | | | | | | |
| Max | | | | | | | |

**4** **Look at Activity 3 and write.**

1  He can __play soccer__, but he can't

_____.

2  She can _____, but she can't

_____.

3  _____, but he can't

_____.

4  Can he _____?

No, _____.

5  _____?

Yes, _____.

**5** Match the sports and places.

(a) basketball court

(b) running track

(c) swimming pool

(d) baseball field

(e) tennis court

(f) soccer field

**6**  Listen and check (✓).

**7** Look at Activity 6 and write *was* or *wasn't*.

**1** He _____ at the baseball field. He _____ at the stadium.

**2** She _____ at the gym. She _____ at the beach.

**3** He _____ at the ski slope. He _____ at the running track.

**8** Write ✓ = can or X = can't.

**9** Write *and* or *but*.

Monkeys can run ¹ _____ jump, ² _____ they can't ride a bike.

They can swim ³ _____ climb trees, ⁴ _____ they can't play tennis.

They can catch a ball, ⁵ _____ they can't play soccer.

**10** Look at Activity 8 and write.

1  He wasn't at the basketball court.

He _____ at the _____.

2  He _____ at the swimming pool.

He _____ at the _____.

3  He _____ gym.

He _____.

4  _____ beach.

_____

5 _____ ski slope.

_____

**11** Look at the story again. Write the things PROD 1 and PROD 2 can and can't do.

> catch   fly   play basketball
> play tennis   ride a bike   run fast   swim

| PROD 1 | PROD 2 |
| --- | --- |
| _____ | _____ |
| _____ | _____ |
| _____ | _____ |
| _____ | _____ |

**12** Look at Activity 11 and write.

1   PROD 1 can play basketball, but he can't run fast.

2   _____

3   _____

4   _____

**13**  **Listen and number. Then write.**

54

Be active. Exercise every day.

**1** go for a walk    **2** do push-ups    **3** do taekwondo

**4** run    **5** ride my bike    **6** play sports

My name's Jane. I like exercise a lot. I ☐ _____

with my friend Sally. I also ☐ _____.

At night, I ☐ _____ or ☐ _____

with my mother. Sometimes I ☐ _____

at the beach with my brother. And, oh, yes! I

☐ _____, too! I want to be very strong.

**14** **Do you exercise? Write the letter.**

            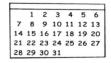

**D = every day**    **W = every week**    **S = sometimes**    **N = never**

**1**  ☐    **2**  ☐    **3**  ☐

**4**  ☐    **5**  ☐    **6**  ☐

**15**  Listen and number.

 a
 b
 c
 d
 e

**16** Make an exercise plan. Write.

> dance    do taekwondo    go to the gym    play baseball
> play basketball    play soccer    play tennis    ride a bike
> run    swim    walk

**My exercise plan**

| Monday | dance |
|---|---|
| Tuesday | |
| Wednesday | |
| Thursday | |

| Friday | |
|---|---|
| Saturday | |
| Sunday | |

**17** Write about your exercise plan.

On Monday, I _____. On Tuesday, I _____.

_____

_____

_____

**18** **Read the words. Circle the pictures.**

flag   glass   sleep   slip

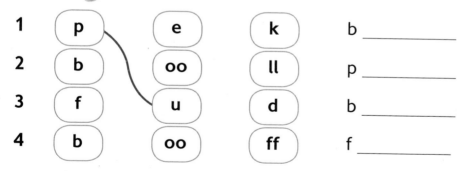

bl   fl   gl
pl   sl

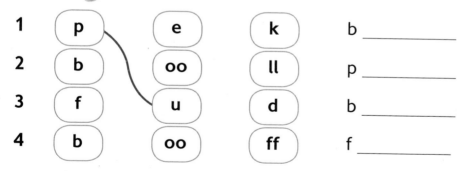

**19** **Listen and connect the letters. Then write.**

| 1 | p | e | k | b _____ |
| 2 | b | oo | ll | p _____ |
| 3 | f | u | d | b _____ |
| 4 | b | oo | ff | f _____ |

**20** **Listen and write the words.**

1 _____   2 _____   3 _____   4 _____

**21** **Read aloud. Then listen and say.**

Look at the ship with the black flag. One man slips. Look out for that shark!

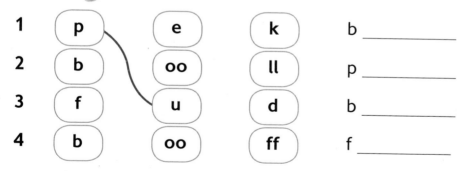

**22** Write ✓ = can or ✗ = can't.

Ted

Sue

Lee

Liz

**23** Look at Activity 22 and write.

1  Can Ted play baseball and ride a bike?  <u>He can't play baseball, but he can ride a bike.</u>

2  Can Sue play tennis and basketball? _____

_____

3  Can Lee _____ and _____? _____

_____

4  Can Liz _____? _____

_____

**24** Write the names of activities that you can or can't do.

| I can | I can't |
|-------|---------|
|       |         |
|       |         |
|       |         |

**25** Look at Activity 24 and write.

1  I can _____, but I can't _____.

2  _____

3  _____

**26** What's your favorite sport? Draw and write or circle.

My favorite sport is _____.

I ( like / don't like ) sports.

I play a sport ( every day / every week ).

I ( sometimes / never ) watch sports on TV.

 **Are you ready for Unit 7?**

# 7 Food

## 1 Match.

1. cucumbers
2. strawberries
3. plums
4. peas
5. tomatoes
6. mangoes
7. oranges
8. carrots
9. potatoes
10. peaches
11. green beans

a

b

c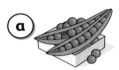

d

e

f

g

h

i

j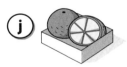

k

## 2 Write about food that you like or don't like.

🙂 I like _____ .

🙁 I don't like _____ .

**3** Listen and ✓ = likes or X = doesn't like.

1 ☐
2 ☐
3 ☐
4 ☐
5 ☐

**4** Look at Activity 3 and write.

1 Does she like plums?
   <u>No, she doesn't.</u>

2 Does she _____ strawberries?
   _____

3 _____ she _____ peas?
   _____

4 _____ he _____ cucumbers?
   <u>Yes, he does.</u>

5 _____ tomatoes?
   _____

**5** **Write Y = Yes or N = No.**

| Tim's house | Are there any...?<br>Is there any...? | Liz's house |
|---|---|---|
| | mangoes | |
| | peaches | |
| | potatoes | |
| | strawberries | |
| | cucumbers | |
| | broccoli | |
| | lettuce | |
| | chicken | |
| | cabbage | |
| | spinach | |
| | cherries | |
| | avocados | |
| | apricots | |
| | pears | |

**6** **Look at Activity 5 and write.**

Tim's house

**1** Are there any pears?

_____

**2** Are there any cherries?

_____

**3** Is there any broccoli?

_____

**4** Is there any lettuce?

_____

Liz's house

**1** Are there any avocados?

_____

**2** Are there any apricots?

_____

**3** Is there any cabbage?

_____

**4** Is there any spinach?

_____

**7**  **Listen and draw a happy face or a sad face.**

**8** **Look at Activity 7 and write.**

**1** Does he like cereal? _____ Yes, he does. _____

**2** Does he like strawberries? _____

**3** Does he like eggs and toast? _____

**4** Does he like peaches? _____

**5** _____ bananas? Yes, he does.

**6** _____ avocados? No, he doesn't.

**9** **Draw food items. Then write your own questions and answers.**

| Fruit | | |
|---|---|---|
| | **1** Are there any _____? Yes, there are. | |
| | **2** Is there any _____? No, there isn't. | |
| | **3** Are there any _____? _____ | |
| | **4** Is there any _____? _____ | |
| | **5** _____ Yes, _____. | |
| Vegetables | **6** _____ No, _____. | |

**10** **Look at the story again. Write.**

**1** Kim, do you like _____ ?

**2** Yuck! No, I _____ like eggs!

**3** Hooray! I _____ tifftiff plants!

**4** Hee, hee! He _____ like tifftiff plants!

**11** **Draw food you like below YUM and food you don't like below YUCK. Then write.**

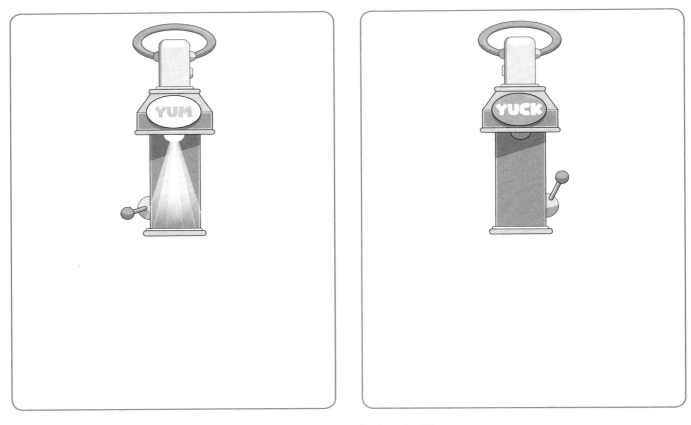

I like _____ .

I don't like _____ .

**12**  **Listen and read. Then underline the unhealthy food items.**

 Stay healthy. Eat more fruit and vegetables.

My name's Millie. I eat healthy food every day. For breakfast, I have fruit juice and cereal. For lunch, I have a sandwich. I don't like burgers. I like rice, green vegetables, and carrots. For dinner, I eat chicken and salad, but sometimes I have pizza and fries. I eat fruit every day, but I like candy, too!

**13** **Write.**

| Healthy food/drinks | | Unhealthy food/drinks | |
|---|---|---|---|
| I like | I don't like | I like | I don't like |
| _____ | _____ | _____ | _____ |
| _____ | _____ | _____ | _____ |
| _____ | _____ | _____ | _____ |
| _____ | _____ | _____ | _____ |

**14** **Look at Activity 13 and write.**

1   What is your favorite healthy food? _____

2   What is your favorite healthy drink? _____

3   What is your favorite unhealthy food? _____

4   What is your favorite unhealthy drink? _____

**15** Match.

**1**

**a** fruit and vegetables

**2**

**3**

**b** dairy

**4**

**5**

**c** proteins

**6**

**7**

**d** fats and sugars

**8**

**9**

**e** grains

**10**

**16** Draw three healthy meals.
Use food from the healthy eating plate.

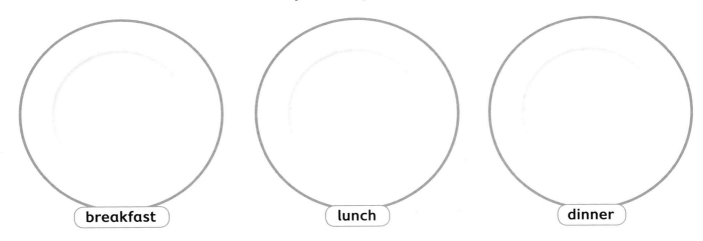

breakfast          lunch          dinner

**17** Look at Activity 16 and write.

For breakfast, I like _____.

For lunch, I like _____.

For dinner, I like _____.

**18** **Read the words. Circle the pictures.**

crab    frog    string    train

| br | cr | dr | fr |
|----|----|----|----|
| gr | pr | str | tr |

**19** **Listen and connect the letters. Then write.**

1    k    ar    ss    w _____

2    w    i    k    g _____

3    sh    e    l    sh _____

4    g    ir    b    k _____

**20** **Listen and write the words.**

1  _____    2  _____    3  _____    4  _____

**21** **Read aloud. Then listen and say.**

The boy likes his toy train. He can pull it with the string. He has a green frog, a brown owl, and a red crab.

**22** **Write.**

Across →

Down ↓

1

2

3

4

5

6

7

8

2

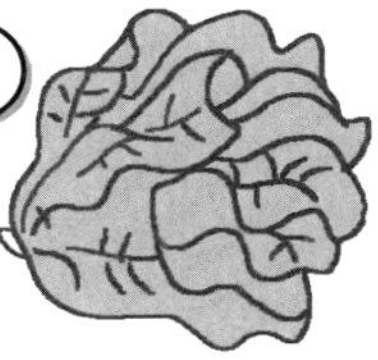

4

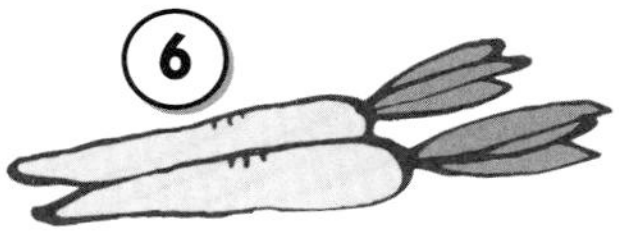

1

6

8

3

5

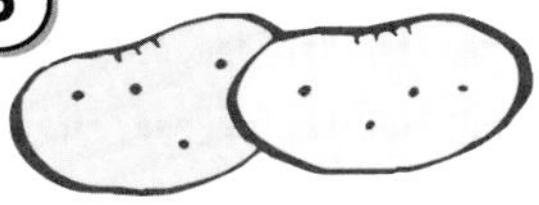

7

**23** **Write.**

1   Does he like mangoes? _____

2   _____ strawberries?

   _____

3   Does she like apricots? _____

4   _____ spinach?

   _____

**24** **Draw food items.**

**25** **Look at Activity 24 and write.**

**1** There's some _____ .

**2** There are some _____ .

**3** _____

**4** _____

**5** Is there any cereal? _____

**6** Are there any strawberries? _____

**26** **Write about your family and friends.**

**1** My friend likes __peaches__ . She doesn't like __apricots__ .

**2** _____

**3** _____

**4** _____

 **Are you ready for Unit 8?**

# 8 Things we do

**1** Listen and number.

a

b

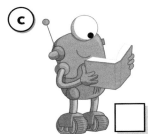
c

d

e

f

g

h

i

**2** Look at Activity 1 and write.

cleaning   dancing   doing homework   drinking   sleeping   walking

Picture a _____

Picture b _____

Picture d _____

Picture f _____

Picture h _____

Picture i _____

**3** 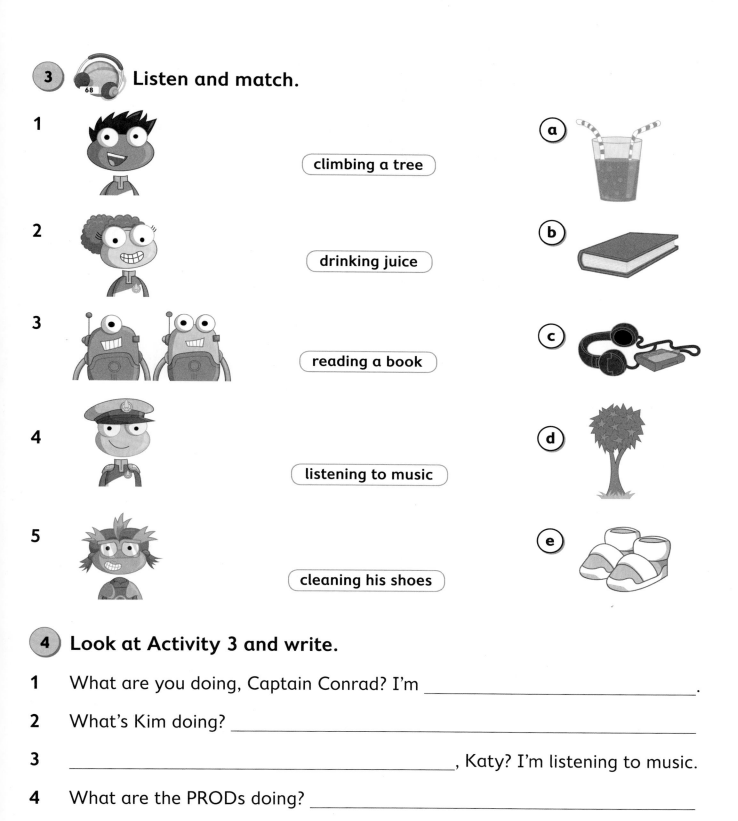 **Listen and match.**

1    climbing a tree      a   (juice)

2    drinking juice      b   (book)

3    reading a book      c   (headphones)

4    listening to music      d   (tree)

5    cleaning his shoes      e   (shoes)

**4** **Look at Activity 3 and write.**

1   What are you doing, Captain Conrad? I'm _____.

2   What's Kim doing? _____

3   _____, Katy? I'm listening to music.

4   What are the PRODs doing? _____

5   What's the trickster doing? He's _____.

**5**  **Listen and check (✓).**

1 Marie ☐ Jenny ☐  2 Ken ☐ Ben ☐  3 Karl ☐ John ☐

4 Kelly ☐ Ann ☐

5 Tim ☐ Pete ☐

**6** **Look at Activity 5 and write.**

> loudly   playing the piano   playing the violin   quickly

1 Are you _____, Marie? Yes, I am.

2 Is Ben playing the flute? No, he isn't. He's _____.

3 Is John _____ terribly? Yes, he is.

4 Are you playing the trumpet slowly, Ann?

_____

5 Is Pete singing quietly?

_____

**7**  **Listen and write.**

Hi, Jason!

I'm in Thailand, and it's very hot! I'm ¹ _____ ice cream by the swimming pool. My sister's swimming ² _____, and Mom's reading ³ _____. My dad's ⁴ _____ to music and singing ⁵ _____, but he's funny. I'm having fun! See you soon!

Adam

To: Jason Spade
    10 Park Street
    New York
    NY 10013
    United States

**8** **Write.**

> **playing the piano   quickly   reading   walking**

1  _____ sleeping?

No, _____. _____

2  Is _____?

Yes, _____.

3  Is _____ slowly?

No, _____. _____

**9** **Write.**

What's she _____?

_____ gardening.

What's _____?

He's running _____.

What _____ doing?

They're going home.

**10** **Write.**

| are    flying    going    listening    reading |

Captain Conrad's ¹ _____ the spaceship. They're ² _____ home.

Katy's ³ _____ a book about plants. Kim's ⁴ _____ to  music.

PROD 1 and PROD 2 ⁵ _____ sleeping.

**11** **Write.**

birthday   cleaning   cookies
favorite   sing   teacher   violin

I'm Danica. I love to learn new things. I can dance, and I can ¹ _____. I have a great music ² _____ at school.

Cooking is my ³ _____ thing to do at home. My mom and I make ⁴ _____ and cake on weekends. I like to cook, but I'm not very good at ⁵ _____ the kitchen!

I can play the piano, but I can't play the ⁶ _____. I want a violin for my ⁷ _____. Then I can learn a new talent!

**12** **Check (✓). Then draw the skill you want to learn.**

| Things I can do | |
| --- | --- |
| dancing | |
| singing | |
| acting | |
| painting | |
| cooking | |
| playing the piano | |
| playing basketball | |
| playing soccer | |
| riding a bike | |

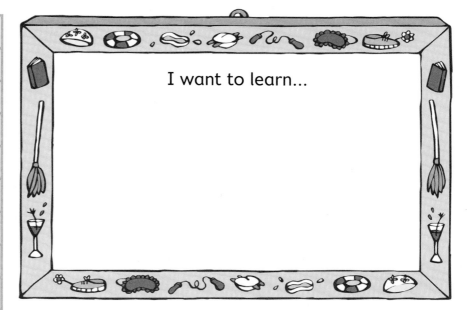

I want to learn...

**13**   Listen, draw, and color.

**14** Write about the airplane.

airplane    flying    pilot    quickly    windows    wings

This is an airplane. It's ¹ _____ in the sky. It can fly very ² _____. It's white. It has two ³ _____. A ⁴ _____ is flying the plane. There are a lot of ⁵ _____. There are 100 people in the ⁶ _____. Do you like to fly?

**15** Read the words. Circle the pictures.

bump   hand   paint   wind

ft   mp   nd   nt
sk   sp   st

**16** Listen and connect the letters. Then write.

1   qu   e   z      b _____

2   y   i   zz      y _____

3   b   ow   n      qu _____

4   d   u   s      d _____

**17** Listen and write the words.

1 _____   2 _____   3 _____   4 _____

**18** Read aloud. Then listen and say.

The painter is up the ladder. The pot goes down with a bump, and the paint goes splat on the man. What a mess!

**19** **Write.**

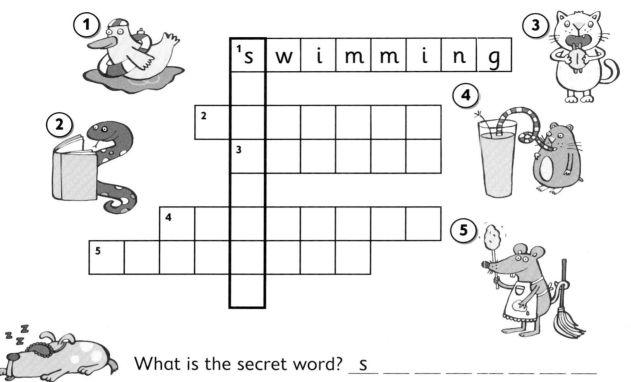

|   | ¹s | w | i | m | m | i | n | g |
|---|---|---|---|---|---|---|---|---|
| 2 |   |   |   |   |   |   |   |   |
| 3 |   |   |   |   |   |   |   |   |
| 4 |   |   |   |   |   |   |   |   |
| 5 |   |   |   |   |   |   |   |   |

What is the secret word? _s_ __ __ __ __ __ __ __

**20** **Write.**

What are you doing?

1 I'm playing the piano.

2 _____

3 _____

4 _____

**21** Write.

**\*\*Talent Show\*\***

Anna

Dan

Eddie

Gigi

Sandy and Amy

Mike and Fred

**1**  What's Eddie doing?  _____

**2**  What are Sandy and Amy doing?  _____

**3**  What's Anna doing?  _____

**4**  What are Mike and Fred doing?  _____

**5**  What's Dan doing?  _____

**6**  What's Gigi doing?  _____

**22** **Draw you in the Talent Show. Then write.**

TALENT SHOW

What are you doing?

I'm _____

_____

_____.

# Goodbye

**1** **Where's the tifftiff plant? Find and write.**

~~above~~  in  behind  below  in front of  next to  on  above

The tifftiff plant is _____ the water.

It's _____ her feet.

It's _____ Kim.

It's _____ the shelf.

It's _____ the jeans.

It's _____ PROD 2.

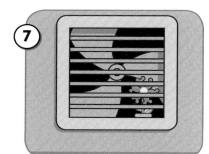

It's _above_ the restaurant.

It's _____ Katy!

## 2 Read and number.

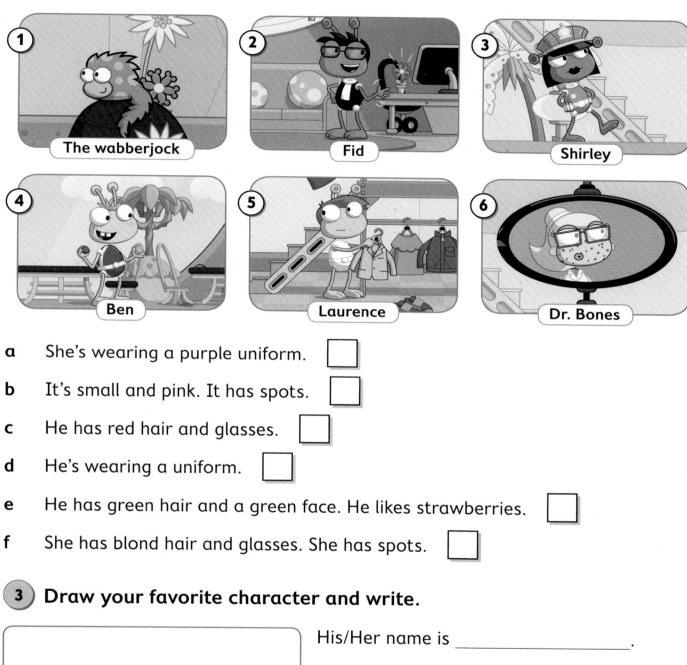

1. The wabberjock
2. Fid
3. Shirley
4. Ben
5. Laurence
6. Dr. Bones

a   She's wearing a purple uniform. ☐

b   It's small and pink. It has spots. ☐

c   He has red hair and glasses. ☐

d   He's wearing a uniform. ☐

e   He has green hair and a green face. He likes strawberries. ☐

f   She has blond hair and glasses. She has spots. ☐

## 3 Draw your favorite character and write.

His/Her name is _____.

He/She has _____.

He's/She's wearing _____.

He/She can _____.

He/She likes _____.

**4** Write about the picture.

There's _____

_____.

There are _____

_____

_____

_____.

**5** Listen and check (✓). Then write.

☐　　　　☐　　　　☐

This is my pet [1] _____. Its name is Pauli. It has colorful [2] _____
and a sharp [3] _____. It has two strong [4] _____. It has sharp
[5] _____. Be careful!

**6** Write things that are in your house.

| Bedroom | Bathroom | Living Room | Kitchen |
|---|---|---|---|
| _____ | _____ | _____ | _____ |
| _____ | _____ | _____ | _____ |
| _____ | _____ | _____ | _____ |

**7** Write about a family member or friend.

| He/She can... | He/She can't... |
|---|---|
| 1 _____ | 1 _____ |
| 2 _____ | 2 _____ |
| 3 _____ | 3 _____ |

**8** What are they doing? Write.

1 _____  2 _____  3 _____  4 _____

**9** Choose and write.

I like _____

and _____.

I don't like _____

and _____.

My friend likes _____

and _____.

My friend doesn't like _____

and _____.

## Welcome

| | |
|---|---|
| **What's** your **favorite day**? | My **favorite day** is Sunday. |

| | |
|---|---|
| **When** were you **born**? | I was **born** in January. |
| Were you **born** in May? | Yes, I was. |
| | No, I wasn't. I was born in June. |

**wasn't = was not**

## Unit 1 Nature

| | |
|---|---|
| How many animals **are there**? | **There's** one purple animal. |
| How many birds **are there**? | **There are** two blue birds. |

| | |
|---|---|
| There are **some** spiders. | There aren't **any** spiders. |
| Is there **a** rainbow? | Yes, there is. / No, there isn't. |
| Is there **any** wind? | Yes, there's **some** wind. / No, there isn't **any** wind. |
| Are there **any** ants? | Yes, there are. / No, there aren't. |

| | |
|---|---|
| **Where** are they? | **At** the library. |
| **Where** is he? | **At** the museum. |

## Unit 2 Me

| I | **have** | glasses. |
|---|---|---|
| | **don't have** | |
| He She | **has** | dark eyebrows |
| | **doesn't have** | |

| **Do** you **have** | long eyelashes? | **Yes**, I **do**. |
|---|---|---|
| | | **No**, I **don't**. |
| **Does** he/ she **have** | curly hair? | **Yes**, he/she **does**. |
| | | **No**, he/she **doesn't** |

## Unit 3 Pets

| What | does it / do they | look like? |
|---|---|---|
| It | has / doesn't have | a tail. / wings. |
| They | have / don't have | whiskers. / fins. |

| Do you have a dog? | Yes, I do. It's cute. / No, I don't. | Does it have soft fur? | Yes, it does. / No, it doesn't. |
|---|---|---|---|

## Unit 4 Home

| There's a plant / There are two plants | in the living room. |
|---|---|
| The plant is/It's / The plants are/They're | below the mirror. |

| Is the computer in the bedroom? | Yes, it is. / No, it isn't. It's in the living room. | Are the plates on the shelf? | Yes, they are. / No, they aren't. They're in the sink. |
|---|---|---|---|

## Unit 5 Clothes

| What are you wearing? | I'm wearing | a baseball cap. |
|---|---|---|
| What's he/she wearing? | He's/She's wearing | sandals. |

| Are you wearing / Is he/she wearing | a baseball cap? / sandals? | Yes, I am. / No, I'm not. / Yes, he/she is. / No, he/she isn't. |
|---|---|---|

| This is | my favorite | scarf. |
|---|---|---|
| These are | | tights. |
| I love my scarf/tights. | | |

## Unit 6 Sports

| I/He/She | can/can't | run and jump. |
| | | run, but I/he/she can't jump. |
| Can you/he/she play tennis? | Yes, | I/he/she | can. |
| | No, | | can't. |

| I/He/She | was at the gym. |
| | wasn't at the gym. I/He/She was at the baseball field. |

## Unit 7 Food

| Do you | | | Yes, I do. |
| | like | peas? | No, I don't. |
| Does he/she | | | Yes, he/she does. |
| | | | No, he/she doesn't. |

| Is there any broccoli? | Yes, there is. |
| | No, there isn't. |
| Are there any pears? | Yes, there are. |
| | No, there aren't. |

## Unit 8 Things we do

| What are you | | I'm | |
| What are they | doing? | They're | sleeping. |
| What's he/she | | He's/She's | |

| Are you singing? | Yes, I am. / No, I'm not. |
| Is he/she singing? | Yes, he/she is. / No, he/she isn't. |
| Is he/she singing quietly? | Yes, he/she is. |
| | No, he/she isn't. He's/She's singing loudly. |